<u>Wisdom 45 Advice</u>

Dorian S. Withrow Jr.

ISBN

Paperback: 979-8-9865238-2-8

Hardcover: 979-8-9865238-4-2

E-Book: 979-8-9865238-9-7

Publisher: Dorian S. Withrow Jr. / Withrow, LLC

Table of Contents

Contact

Author: Dorian S. Withrow Jr.

Social media: Instagram, Tik Tok, Twitter

- **@dswjr.18**

Website

- **www.dswjr.com**

Email

- **114realities@gmail.com**

Illustrator: Bree Gilliam

Social media: Instagram

- **@breegilliamart**

Website

- **www.breegilliam.com**

Email

- **breegilliamart@gmail.com**

What is this book about?

This book is about self-improvement through life lessons and philosophy. My lived experiences bring relatability and value. I applied philosophical concepts, such as skepticism and stoicism. I want to use those in a way to combat sorrow, anger, anxiety, and more. There are poetic elements to this book as well. These poetic elements bring more creativity and a much more exciting delivery. I want people to consider how they can create meaning in life, what it takes to make progress, and how to find out who they are. I want to help people make changes. People will become vulnerable and get motivated. People can discover their aspirations and more inspiration. Readers will establish visions, set goals, improve their communication, and take account of their influences. In addition, they will also learn how to deal with friends and pressure. People may even smile more and develop increased capital.

I am Dorian

I am wise and generous,

I wonder about the fruits I've planted.

I hear the voices of the heavens in my ears.

I see the paradise I am making.

I want what I prayed for.

I am wise and generous.

I pretend to live in the success I envision.

I feel the whispering winds blowing advice.

I touch the earth that nourishes me.

I worry about the troubled,

I cry over their sorrow,

I am wise and generous.

I understand my assigned task.

I say perfection is what is now.

I dream about the ill's fading,

I try to educate willing ears,

I hope there will be little need for this later.

I am wise and generous.

Know Yourself

The most dangerous and threatening person in the world is yourself! No one else has or ever will have more control over you than yourself. You can conquer almost anything you know best. People must take more time out of their everyday lives to ponder who they are. That is, your character, integrity, generosity, humility, respectfulness, troubles, talents, etc. You should have an honest internal monologue about values as well. Honesty is the best way to find the truth and what needs to be adjusted. Other people can also be a resource for discovering the truth about yourself. But be careful; not everyone will have an honest view of you. Do not emulate others; let them be a lesson to help you find yourself. They can help expose your limits to various things, like conviction. Others can challenge your resilience, confidence, and disposition. In this way, people can learn about themselves. Knowing yourself also means understanding your heritage. Your family tree will not dictate who you are, but it can be a reference point or stepping stone to changing your perception of yourself. It would help if you took pride in the positive aspects of your heritage and what it encompasses. Explore religion, ritual, clothing, and philosophies. In addition, when opportunities present themselves, take them. Opportunities are chances to expose yourself to something that may guide your development and discovery. You never know what opportunities might bring. Also, act on your interests. You may encounter a situation or circumstances that will show you your beliefs may not be what you thought they were. You only know what you like or dislike once you try it. For whatever comes to you, examine how it changes your being. You may get into spaces where you can reach authenticity. We live in a world that demands a mask and filtered thoughts. A perfect way to know yourself is to be yourself through pure self-expression. Put yourself in spaces around people you do not have to hide from.

Friends

Knowing yourself will help you determine your social circles. Friends are the people that you go to for advice. The people you share your accomplishments with. They are the people you trust with confidentiality and aim to help you improve. More importantly, they are the people who do not seek to harm you mentally or physically, whether or not it be in a "joking manner." Friends that do harm is an issue that comes up very often. People consider friends who talk down to them or go a bit over the top to challenge them physically. Those people should be reconsidered heavily. Is the relationship delightful and supportive or negative and depressing? Success is a great test to determine who to hang around. When you tell that friend about your accomplishments, read their response (verbal and physical). Furthermore, we are human beings! We make mistakes, hold negative preconceived notions, and deal with our bad habits. Our bad habits and destructive mentalities could be detrimental to relationships without realizing it.

When that friend knows you are wrong, will they correct you? Are they willing to say what no one else will? A friend will not reinforce, influence, or promote harm. A friend is willing to put the friendship on the line for improvement. Moreover, differences in opinion, values, and beliefs are needed, but an open mind is even better. Diversity of thought can open people up to seeing themselves concerning the world differently. They can help you foster a new or slightly changed way of thinking. Many ideas are better than one. Also, we ought to know the purpose of friendship and let it be for a good reason. Sometimes, the hard truth behind wanting "friends" is that people are lonely. Lonely people might seek many friends, whether good or bad. Some people use friends to fulfill their emotional needs. Some want to feel superior to another or have someone around to feel needed. There are many moral and ethical problems with this. Some seek to use friends to get ahead in life. They'll use anyone of value. When we choose friends, we have to have people around for the right reasons. It is relevant for us to put people in our circles because of who they are as human beings. The benefit that comes with them is a bonus. This makes our relationships meaningful and worthwhile.

Rise Above

According to the Greek philosopher Diogenes, society is "mad." The difference in people's reactions between using our most extended finger and our pinky demonstrates the mad society. Walk around with the middle finger extended, and you will receive a variety of destructive emotions and foul attention. It is only a finger, but some people will lose their minds. Walk around with the pinky extended, and you'll receive little attention. No matter what finger is directed at us, we must rise above. The philosopher Epictetus' control concept can be applied here. You can only manage yourself. You control your actions, thoughts, and behaviors. When treated poorly, some people will consider reacting negatively first. In all cases, we should maintain good character. One should always say thank you as needed, even if you heard the worst thing in the world, and smile like you have seen the sunshine for the first time. Let them know you can not be affected and show strength. People can say what they want and do what they will, but it is best to be your best version of yourself. If they attack you verbally, then consider it harmless in some cases. Words are not bullets unless you make them. Language is a powerful thing. Certain people have good management of profanity, while others do not. You need to have self-control and rise above that. Think of that as beneath you; people of your stature do not absorb that behavior. It is unattractive, lowers yourself, and changes other people's perceptions of you. If someone attacks you physically, defend yourself and involve the law. If avoidable, steer clear of conflict completely. Police are here to handle things like that, and the courts are here to sort out right and wrong. Meanwhile, you have to consider your image in the public setting. What people think of us matters directly and indirectly. Some people think they are beyond this, but no one is. People in that public space could play a part in your future. They could dictate what doors open for you or don't. We are human, but responding harshly only if needed is better. Like fire fought with fire, sometimes it is better if the flame isn't exacerbated. Some bridges don't have to be crossed; some paths don't have to be walked. In the end, choose the course of action that benefits all. Reconciliation is a significant step we very often neglect. Pride and ego may get in the way; that must be checked. You can only check your pride and ego. We have to reevaluate the way we approach a terrible interaction. Think about what you could have done differently. Did my temper get in the way of de-escalating the situation? You may have improved. Ask yourself, how did they help you as a person? After the event occurs, reshape the experience into a lesson. Focus on what you learned. We all benefit from something terrible, but we have to find it. What helps me is maintaining focus on the finish line, the end goal. Whatever the altercation, act in accordance with meeting the finish line (the best outcome). It means a level of strength, maturity, and discipline most people do not have. More importantly, prevent yourself from becoming worse. Rise above the trivial by showing you can't be affected and don't become it.

Peer Pressure

Peer pressure is something we learn young and constantly experience at all ages. Our elders, parents, and teachers tell us not to fall to peer pressure. My great-grandmother would say, "If you know something ain't right, get out of there." My father would tell me, "Do not follow the wrong crowd." and my teacher used to say, "If you see something bad, do not copy it." People of all ages value their relationships with others. Sometimes, people value relationships more than themselves, thus making them more susceptible to being influenced or pressured. I define peer pressure as being influenced to behave or think in a way against your inclinations. Knowing right and wrong is not enough. To fight against peer pressure, someone must have the mental fortitude, resilience, and indomitable stubbornness of their values, beliefs, and morals. This creates the ability to prevent ourselves from being swayed by beautiful words. When people know themselves, they know what will incline them to be influenced by peer pressure.

People have to reflect and tackle what troubles them. People must also be informed of negative influences in a relationship. A bond can blind us, but it is strong enough to say "no." A reasonable person can get into dire circumstances by following the wrong person. Negative activity goes against your decency, integrity, values, and well-being. This can happen to anyone of any status. If you are peer pressured, then find different friends and associates. Those people do not have your best interest at heart. They are pressing their reflection of their own best interest at heart. Find a different workspace, groups, people, and class areas, and make internal changes.

Go Beyond

Look below to see,

Leave behind poor energy,

Focus on the new.

Smile

Smiling is something I had to learn. I thought it wasn't genuine and lying to an extent if I had to smile on command. I have a relaxed face most of the time. My face may appear serious or whatever false emotion people muster when a situation arises. Smiling on command is something I am still working on. Some people have a resting, "stay away" face. People may perceive it as angry, serious, or sad. Therefore, you could be more appealing and approachable. We have to wrinkle the corners of our eyes and raise the corners of our mouths. With practice, I and the other facial expression managers lie to everyone through our expressions. Thank you society! Smiling is an excellent tool for development. Smiling is what makes us more appealing and attractive. Smiling is a magnet to joyful emotion and creating a good experience for people. People will remember you as being much happier. Smiling applies to any social gathering, entrepreneurial venture, public speaking, video production, or business opportunity. Smiling works. Smiling raises your social and monetary capital. It is a piece of the puzzle that builds the picture of success. Even when you are having a bad day, smile not just for other people but for yourself. Think about what will bring joy. Many things bring me joy. I think of a happy experience, the joke I couldn't get out of my head. Think of the amazing conversation you had with your loved ones. Find music that brings you to that exciting space. I listen to music that instills confidence and an excited mood. Music has a potent influence on what we think, how we think, and how we feel. Be careful what you listen to. Lastly, I love listening to comedy. To me, a good laugh can throw away a thousand bad days. Smiling is also a tool to use against wicked people. The wicked people want to get under your skin, harm you, and into your head. Show them you are unfazed by smiling. You can not be hurt or broken. Smile and walk away from pointless arguments. Become a good actor. You are above, remember that.

Money

An abundance of money could mean no more financing, flexibility, leisure, little to no debt, and less stress. How you manage your dollars is more important than how many dollars you have. It is essential to save the cash you get. Spend a lot less than what you earn. Without assets, avoid debt, but if unavoidable, manage debt well. The objective of this financial world is to make more return than loss of earnings. Furthermore, we must invest in the correct information: your connections, inner circle, and network matters. Seek and learn from people winning in the financial realm and other areas. Always learn before you engage in any financial venture. Also, we must find a way to create assets by developing products, methods, and/or services that allow us to gain income. It will help us increase our revenue. Our unique abilities can make it happen. I use my talent and passion to make my contribution to society. I co-authored my first literary work, *Speak Young Brown People, Speak. We Are Listening!* I can print the books and sell them. I developed an asset when I published my second book, *Thought of Creativity King 114 Realities*. The book is a route for entrepreneurship and more income opportunities. I no longer have to work on the book, retyping, resetting graphics, etc. This is the current milestone I am in. I am excited, nervous, happy, concerned, and curious about what position I will place myself in. Recently, I thought of helping others become authors as someone did for me. I started Withrow, LLC, an author consulting business. I give thorough, informative sessions with resources through a step-by-step process to become self-published. What I provide can be seen on my website, dswjr.com. Please create your asset and turn it into much more. What will bring money in? Society has problems, groups of people have issues, and nature has problems. What can you produce or serve to help people get past or around their difficulties? Furthermore, one thing I wished I learned about was personal finance; not just personal finance, but taxes, retirement, and types of investments. The youth should take time to seek out information with guidance and good judgment.

Gut Feeling

One of the most prominent pieces of advice my great-grandmother gave me was to trust your gut feeling. She spoke of my great uncle, who had a form of that "gut feeling." She'd say, "Your great uncle would get a burning sensation on his neck. When something was not feeling right, he would get that burning feeling. "Doe, doe's (what she called me) find that gut feeling and listen to it." Regarding myself, it is similar to a feeling of sudden worry or concern, a voice in my head telling me to do or not to do something. When I follow that voice, the outcomes will sometimes turn out well. When I don't follow that voice, sometimes I experience misfortune. I followed my gut feeling to my literary work, financial decisions, martial arts, and college; it has been fruitful so far. The gut feeling told me to persevere, explore, try, and complete. Find your "gut feeling". I believe it will help you daily.

Confidence and Self Esteem

I have learned that we are the most dangerous threat to ourselves. There is also nothing more precious in the world than yourself. No one else can destroy us faster than ourselves, and no one will help you nourish yourself better than you. Low confidence and low self-esteem are development killers. We all have things we consider wrong with us. It may be reading, weight, body parts, social life, and money. Low confidence and self-esteem will tell you to close the doors of opportunity when it opens. I have some confidence and esteem boosters. I make the most of my achievements and rewards visible somewhere. On one wall in my room is a small monument with a banner from the college where I graduated and the medals I earned from competitive tournaments. I also have all the belts I earned in a wooden case. I have a newspaper that has an article about me. There's a meddle from an essay contest. I even have a picture from elementary school with a title I earned, "Creativity King." My second book is called *Thoughts Of Creativity King 114 Realities.* I have a plethora of achievement folders from programs my mother involved me in. Build your achievement collection or, as I say, a "Wall of Rewards." Having rewards visible reminds us of where we are going and how far we've come. If you do not have that many or none, there are ways to go about it! You can receive many rewards by volunteering, participating in workshops, martial arts, dancing, singing, or participating in a progressive group. It's best to engage in something that will give your life meaning. Knowing that you are making a change within yourself or in someone's life and/or community is what develops us. You will walk a different way with more confidence in your speech. It also helps to focus on creating more goals. You will constantly begin to envision the results of our labor. It's important to remember that vision is nothing without action. You have to go to war with your troubles. If our trouble is weight, exercise appropriately, manage time, and diet reasonably. If reading is an issue, research what you like and read about it often. Progress is not always easy, so when action gets hard, find motivation. Find that thing or person to get you moving. I look at people excelling and proficient in the realms I aim for. I set a plan to have goals and a method to the finish line. When there is a plan in place, there is a direction. Be consistent in what you are striving for. Also, one of the biggest influences on our confidence and self-esteem is people. Everyone needs a coach and/or accountability partner. This person will help you get the goal met and overcome inevitable challenges. Take the good and leave out the bad in all advice. Embrace the good and recall it when times get tough. Know that the seemingly impossible is within your reach. You won't know until you try. On the negative side, when someone mocks you for trying your best to become exceptional, you know you are on the right path. They are watching you for a good reason, but their words could be intentionally harmful. How will you grow if you are around people trying to reduce you? Build your conscience further by being around positive people with positive words. Get in front of the mirror to see every centimeter of perfection you were gifted. See that love within yourself internally and externally. Talk yourself up throughout the day. Fill your brain with constant positivity, motivation, and inspiration. Contemplate your qualities and beauty. Every day, find a little more of your gold and remove your burden. We are perfect; we must see it outside of our prejudice. Live a life you are proud of. Often, you should look back and be happy about what you've done. Lastly, be careful when seeking validation from others regarding anything about yourself. People give their perspective of you through their filtered world. Whatever your talents, aspirations, achievements, or improvements, always know it within yourself. Some people do not believe in you or see the vision you have.

Self

Mirrors are perfect,
The mind fogs perfection,
Meditate, wash it.

Skepticism

I want to shape skepticism in a way to combat worry or concern. Skepticism is a branch of philosophy. It is an area originally used for objects of sense and objects of thought, good and evil. Skeptics wanted to see if objects are as they appear. The Philosopher and skeptic Sextus Empiricus can teach us something about worry. I want to do this through equipollence, mental suspense, and quietude. When we worry about anything, it can induce stress, anxiety, and even depression. Often, we want to find an answer to something or someone. We can get entangled in the web of possible answers. This can be nerve-racking and sleep-depriving. Sometimes, there is no answer, or we may be better off without one. To save yourself some hair, employ equipollence in appropriate contexts. Equipollence is to hold something equally in likelihood. We want to cancel out whatever the probability of the given concern. It is neither true nor untrue. When you do this, you do not get any closer to the answer, but you're trying to avoid looking for an answer. When we have no answer, it takes away concern. (In philosophy, the skeptics keep searching). We want to prevent ourselves from becoming dogmatic. To be dogmatic is to think you have found the truth and hold it absolute. In addition, what seems to help when confronted with a situation like this is (the battle between truth and untrue) to avoid assumptions. Assumptions are simply making up an uncertain answer. Assumptions can place you into anxiety and a bad emotional state. You can hold the wrong preconceived judgments before knowing the truth. An assumption may bring on more harm than good when wrong. The weight of an assumption could lead to a lot of trouble. Sometimes there is no answer. Worry less and reach a state of mental suspense. We do not know now, so let's put our minds at ease. Let it leave your mind altogether or at least lessen the burden. We can focus our minds elsewhere. Keep a healthy concentration on goals or objectives you want completed. Examine what habits you want broken or productive habits you want to develop. We have to get rid of the junk from our minds. We are then guided into quietude, that is, to be calm, unbothered, and reach a tranquil state of mind. Through this, we can limit the troubles of concern and worry in many circumstances.

Respect the Elders

The wisest thing I did was to respect my good elders. I would listen to my great-grandmother, mother, and father. My great-grandmother was a religious woman who always had biblical references. She always brought morality into conversation and stories when she talked to me. At a young age, I stood before her, listening for hours. At that time, it almost seemed like torture. As of today, it bore more fruit than I was aware of. Moreover, my mother started talking in the manner that my great-grandmother did. I felt like I went back in time. It was as if they switched rolls. She usually talked about the right way to do things as it was on her mind. My father would start his moral lessons whenever a situation came up. When I listened to them at a young age, they gave

me guidelines, developed my character, and helped
me establish my position in life. Applying the
lessons from your wise elders will save you a lot of
hardship. Those same lessons also taught me how to
navigate hardship. A mistake I see many young
people make now is listening to the wrong people.
Learning from a bad example is detrimental. Find
the elder with a sound mind and good standing in
life. You want people around who make progress.
Appreciate the people who put in effort to help you
become the greatest you. You have an obligation to
shine and let them know. I had shown my mother
the Phi Sigma Tau initiation, the first book I
co-authored, and the second book. I told her about
the St. Thomas Aquinas Award and the Martin
Luther King Jr. award letters. I received the rewards
the day before my undergraduate graduation. Her
skin turned red when she ran through that in her
head, and she bawled her eyes out. All the time,
energy, moods, money, traveling, and much more
she put in helped me become wondrous. Everyone
has this person in their life: that person who wants

you to achieve no matter what and who wants to see you shine. Identify that person! Let them know everything is going right, and everything is going wrong. Think about how grateful you are to have that person in your life. Always consider what they have done for you. Imagine what it must have been like to be in their shoes to support you. You are obligated to shine for them and, more importantly, acknowledge your own glow. Do not let anyone dim your light in the process. Also, remember we all have our problems; learn the good and bad from their way of life. In this way, the younger generation will start having more respect for their elders. We have to show appreciation, and it should be a mutual act. Do not let pride get the best of reciprocating appreciation. Finally, respect comes when there is something to admire deeply. Respect is not intrinsic to anyone. In all cases, it is earned in some way, shape, or form.

Early Bird Gets The Worm

Most differences between people come from their development in their younger years. We learn our valuable lessons young. I have a series of examples from my life that led to my more outstanding outcomes later on. My mother would tell me to do my homework when I came home from school. After hours of sitting in school, I preferred not to do homework. Modern Warfare and Call of Duty were much more appealing. I was instructed not to get up until the schoolwork was finished, and I did it. Likewise, whenever I wanted to go outside or visit a relative, the home needed to be clean. Before engaging with friends, I had to ensure I was ahead of class projects. Furthermore, my parents required that I get in bed early and set clothing aside for the next day. This taught me time management, responsibility, planning, and priorities. Taking care of responsibilities was something constantly instilled within me at a young age. Our teachers and professors tell us to study early for one week's preparation. If you wait until the last minute to study, you won't be ready for the task. Also, our physical education teachers and physicians tell us to exercise every day. We are directed to eat healthy options and stretch daily. Your body will age and weaken over time. Without the steps to maintain your health early, your body will deteriorate faster and worse. On top of that, in my early teens, my grandmother started my life insurance. She tells me young people die every day, and in recent climates, the risk is always present. When she told me that as an adult, it helped me develop my foresight. The foresight is not to look for the worst with paranoia but to build coverage. It led me to consider what I want to leave behind and the kinds of protection I need. It is something I carry with me to this day. The examples of lessons I've gotten are wider than the education system or household. It is a handful of concepts that assist in navigating life. For me, the ability to maintain those lessons is life-changing. While young, handle the work, learn responsibilities, have discipline, and complete your goals. You'll have less regret when you're older.

Progress

People who make significant progress in their lives have a great desire. Some people are driven to become something great and establish their name in stone. People want to accomplish something many others will not achieve. They want to stand outside of the norm. They want to make their specialty known to the world. Drive for progress develops in two ways: aspiration and inspiration. These are compelling tools. Aspiration is a strong desire to complete or be something. Let your aspirations reach the stars and beyond. Aim small, and you'll get small. Aim towards something lofty, and you'll receive a fruitful return when you walk that path. Inspiration is what moves you to reach your aspiration. Inspiration can be anything, including fear, scarcity, people, legacy, hardship, etc. The best out of that list is people. People generally serve as our greatest inspiration through their example of life. Learn yourself and identify your aim in life. Look for those succeeding in what you are aiming for. Let these people be your motivation to achieve your goals. What did they do? How did they start? What are the steps they take every day to make their progress? What principles and values do they live by? We fall short somehow, so remember to take the good without the bad. Find your inspiration to make progress. Study, learn, and work hard to achieve your goal. Do as successful people do with modification and originality. When beginning your journey, it is essential to start, even without direction. Many people do not start at all. Whatever is on your mind can be done. Many inventions and methods began in the mind, and people worked it into existence. At one point, people thought about flying in the sky. We do not fly precisely like birds, but look up often, and you'll see machines. Those machines are products people once thought impossible, but a group made it happen—the same with cell phones, cosmetics, bullet trains, transfusing plasma, and engine lubrication. What do you think can do? Moreover, I want to distinguish between "I will try" and "I will finish." Do not be the person to try; be the "finisher," as my old psychology professor once told me. Be the person to start and follow through no matter what. The best way to keep progressing is to make small progress steps. When you reach milestones, goals become perceivably obtainable. Stand and observe the rocks you place under your feet. Eventually, you will stand on the mountain you have built. On top of that, you are a role model during the journey. People will see your progress and may strive for their own goals; you've become motivation for someone else. Also, do not be content with what you have done. Be happy and delighted you have succeeded. We should constantly acknowledge there is always more to do. There is comfortability when we don't acknowledge there is more. In comfortability, we slow down and even stop striving for more. Therefore, let your discomfort and concerns motivate you to continue. When we are in the process of doing something great, it is not always easy. There will be roadblocks and challenges. Like my father would say, walk with your head up. When doubt creeps in, remember that you can achieve what you direct your mind to. Think positive and ponder the inspiration that fuels you. You owe it to yourself to be competent throughout your process. Furthermore, when we strive for something great, we need help. We have to seek strong people where we are weak. Significantly, we do not entirely rely on others. People may try to discourage you. Some may be incompetent on their end, which may make milestones problematic. Build your resources and connections to supplement your work—finally, my advice to the parents. I attribute my progress to my mother's willingness to see that I can become the best I can be. What she could not get me, she found someone else who could. She had me placed in many programs and places of assistance for my development. In these spaces, I have had many fortunate experiences. I learned about occupations, finances, dance, culture, and more. Within these spaces, I could put my best foot forward. I used that to my advantage, and it led to many achievements. My work ethic within the programs led to more opportunities, confidence, connections, and better character. I have had the chance to explore myself. Through that experience, I have found my strengths and cultivated my mind. Also, within the programs, I have come across many men and women who do amazing things. They are examples of what a good person is. I learn from them and apply them as best I can. This added to my development. In anything you do, take pride in your work, love it, and finish it.

Becoming A Good Man

Becoming a good man requires good role models. Role models are a significant step to being the best you can be. One should have role models of different backgrounds. Everyone has their weaknesses, while others have strengths to combat those shortcomings. The greater the diversity of thought, profession, and education, the more it can add to developing the child's wisdom. To the parents, teaching your boys what a good role model looks like is imperative. If the parents can not, they are to find someone who can. Role models have significant influence over people who follow the model's example. We subscribe to a different definition of a good role model. A good role model lives life in a way conducive to progress. A good model has a lot more good habits than high-intensity bad habits. The role model is willing to teach you and/or lead by example of what to do as a man. This is someone who values the people around him. The role model has a good reputation. This role model preferably serves as a representation of who he is modeling for. The representation can mean better retention of information, stronger bonds, and relatability. The lessons and examples are much more accurate and achievable to the receiver. The most important characteristic of a good role model is discipline. Discipline is what keeps men orderly. Discipline validates the role models' lessons and values. A lesson is devalued when the teacher contradicts it. Young men must continuously evolve their circle of models and teachers who provide something different. Many of my role models came from programs I was involved in during my teen years. A lot of youth programs can bring good role models to the forefront. I benefit greatly from being close to doctors, entrepreneurs, businessmen, lawyers, the wealthy, and other scholars. They are people who fit my representation. It is inspirational at a high level. Whenever I am around those people, I listen attentively and ask questions. I call it success education. If we have access to greatness, we should use the opportunity to become great by learning and applying the knowledge. Also, understand that we have to seek out our path. Our role models can help us aim. I have a mentor I sought out one day. I talked with him about my plans. At the time, I had graduated from high school and was waiting for my introduction to college. I was deciding on what I wanted to do in life. I told him about some of my desired paths even though I was unsure. He asked about my likes, passions, purpose, and what I was good at. We talked a little bit, but I could not find a conclusion. Eventually, an idea clicked when I left. I thought to myself, I can write a book of poetry. I had already written poetry in high school. As time went on, I decided to add to this book. Over the years, my experiences increased, leading to the book being much more unique and developed. My mentor helped me aim my arrow called life path. In all my processes of positioning my arrow, I seek advice and counsel from many people. I look towards the people that have done it well. When I receive advice, it helps me go a long way. The advice given to me is to be patient, ponder artistic aspects, stay consistent, and enjoy the challenges. I applied what I learned to my process. The book became even greater. As my experience came, I wanted to make the book more diverse. I decided to add stories, spoken word, illustrations, and haiku. My contribution to the world is creative, relatable, and exciting literature to bring development and morality. This book is *Thoughts Of Creativity King*

114 Realities, an innovative, creative self-help book. A book that uses life lessons and philosophy to change the mind for development. My role models helped me develop a mind to change my path and provide for society. We have to put the youth in place to find great role models. Programs or facilities that offer unique experiences for the youth are needed. Young people should have a simulation of entrepreneurship and business. In the boys and girls club I attended, college students came to do entrepreneurial activities with us. We were given an objective to make and sell t-shirts. The students walked us through the design and pricing, allowing us to take reasonable reign over the project. I learned a little bit about business through those students. Besides entrepreneurship, young people should know what comes with pursuing secondary and post-secondary education. The youth need to be better informed about debt, majors, and academic responsibilities. The youth need assistance developing their goals and establishing plans to reach their aspirations. I will

leave questions for you: my role model left me.
What will you produce for society? Will society
love and benefit from it? Can you reach
entrepreneurship or business through your
education? What is the need in society, and how can
you fulfill that?

Questioned

I told him to stop crying,

I wondered if his expression turned into destruction.

I had a lack of trust,

I wondered if she'd become cold to me

I told them to stop questioning me,

I wondered If I filled their curiosity.

I saw the worst in me when I got angry,

I wondered if I ended up just like them.

I was afraid,

I wondered if they saw it.

I saw people talk behind each other's back

I wondered if they were really friends

I witnessed two people harm each other.

I wondered if they were family or not.

I notice people flaunting jewelry

I wondered who's net worth was lower

I heard them talk down to each other.

I wondered who's worth was lower.

I made jokes,

I wondered if it killed their self-esteem

I made jokes with them,

I wondered how low we could go.

I acknowledged we all had low self-esteem.

It seemed like our favorite game was limbo.

Others' Greatness

Be proud of other people and do not see them as competitors. Those people should motivate you to develop. Acknowledge your peers and strangers who are achieving great things. To the people growing and transforming things greatly, praise them authentically. These people could be a part of your network and even a stepping stone to reaching your desired destination. The goal for our community should be to elevate everyone in some way. It takes a village to help anyone get to the highest heights. When people achieve their goals, our community should be happy and excited. Other people can teach us that what may be perceived as unachievable is, in fact, achievable. We can then develop a dream, a dream others could not muster. Then, we can live and behave in a way that will motivate others. To reach the communal winning mind starts with us as individuals first. We must consider other people as resources that will help us manage life. We need other people to become greater ourselves. We are gifted with a talent or ability that can be used to elevate other people as well. Build the desire to invest in your knowledge and ability, then help others. Then, we are a resource to others. When others do well, congratulate them. When others do poorly, encourage them to do better. We should still lend a hand even when they are on their path to victory. I had an exciting teacher when I was in early elementary school. He served as a representation for me within the classroom. From what I remember, he worked with me a lot, one on one. During our

breaks or recess, everyone would get up to play in
their groups. I was very slow to write. Most of the
time, I'd stay in my seat and write until I had
finished the objective. It is because I often chose to
do it while watching others play. By the time I was
finished, it was lunchtime. One day, that teacher
told my mother he had something unique about him.
He acknowledged my greatness and worked with
me. He witnessed my young work ethic and
persistence. I had met a lot of people like this man. I
was very grateful for not encountering many people
who would reduce my dream, vision, or aspiring
thoughts. Cherish that person, then fill their shoes.
On the other hand, some people don't acknowledge
your greatness. They will even try to belittle your
accomplishments. When we see people achieving,
do not seek to tear them down. Don't turn every
pebble, search every crevice, and cut down every
blade of grass to find their faults. This will help us
develop a communal winning mind. When we try to
outdo others, it takes our eye off of the ball
(ourselves). The idea that it is us against our

neighbors that leads to communal weakness. This will bring down our development. Jealousy and envy are some of the things that can act as a hindrance to the community. It will cause fragmentation between groups and individuals. It is one more unnecessary, negative aspect that will decay our community.

Vision Board, Five-Year Plan, & What It Takes

I was introduced to vision boards in youth programs. Without a vision, people float aimlessly. The vision board is made up of images that convey our aspirations. We have to be clear about what we are striving for. Significantly, we put the greatest aspirations on our vision board. There should be no limitation or doubt in this process. We must have the self-esteem to say, "I will reach beyond the stars." The last vision board I created at seventeen had Kevin Hart well-dressed. In the future, I want nice clothing. I had a picture of expensive cologne because smelling good was necessary and a dog because it was something I had never had. I had a cut out of the word "father" at the top and center because I want to be the most incredible father I can be. There was a nice car, a lady model, a mansion, and a few other things. If I made one today, my board would be a little different. In those same programs, we sometimes made five-year plans in workshops. A five-year plan is complementary to a vision board. In the five-year plan, we can think through the stepping stones to make the vision board come to life. This is the list of goals we set for ourselves within five years. My five-year plan included getting into a good college. I wanted to be without student loan debt and with some dollars in my pocket. I wanted to have a good woman. My aspiration in the plan was to finish college with good grades and publish a book. I accomplished everything in the five-year plan. In addition to the five-year plan and vision board, we should write "what it takes." This list of things will keep you on track to meet all the goals within the five-year plan. Will it require creating assets, networking, eating healthier, and learning more? Will the list involve more kindness, smiling, and avoiding indulging in the negative? Think about what ideal conditions you can put yourself in or make for yourself. Consider what connections you'll need and so on. When we write out what it takes, we must work on something daily. Lastly, keep the vision board, five-year plan, and a list of what it takes close by. I kept those three things on top of my dresser when I created them. It is a reminder to keep my mind on desired results, milestones, and what it takes to meet them.

Mistakes

Mistakes are unavoidable and never-ending. Mistakes are great teachers and excellent character builders if you learn from them. People can be embarrassed and ashamed to make mistakes. Through embarrassment and shame, we can be gripped by fear. Fear will prevent us from trying. We must overcome those feelings because the rewards are more fruitful when we learn from them. As a young student, I would not raise my hand to questions. I made no attempts to answer questions I did not know out of fear of how I'd be perceived. I would confidently raise my hand for the questions I did know. I had a fear of being seen as ignorant by other students. That would bring embarrassment and shame. I did not want other people to think of me a certain way. As I aged, it became easier to raise my hand for questions I had no answer to. When I raised my hand to answer questions, I didn't know I'd learn more, regardless of whether I was right or wrong. I learned that I was wrong. When you attempt to answer correctly, others will follow up with their take. I learned that there is a correct or different answer through participation from others. My classmates provided a vast amount of unique perspectives and ideas on topics. Through attempting to answer, I learned that education is a collaborative act. The entire room may discover a new approach or answer to a question. Those people who want answers and seek answers grow much more knowledgeable. Overcoming mistakes and ignorance means learning from people around us. Individually, we will not always have the answers.

Furthermore, my experience in ITF Taekwondo taught me a lot about mistakes. My grandmaster continuously reminded us that we will always be working to improve. We will improve, but perfection is just out of reach. I have made more mistakes than I could count. I have also had plenty of embarrassing moments. I have to accept what happened and move on. Like with life, we will make mistakes. At any age, we make mistakes and often repeat them. In a sense, we can be easier on ourselves. Life does not come with a manual. When you learn something, retain it well and pass it on to help people avoid making mistakes. We can grow at a high level. Also, acknowledge history. One of the greatest lessons I was given was from my great-grandmother. She always told me to learn from those who came before me. She put it in the context of family, but I want to modify it to the context of humanity. People, past or present, are a great resource to prevent mistakes. I encourage us to observe others, listen, and read about others' experiences and issues. We can learn what puddles to avoid. Next, I learned a precious lesson in college. Poor performance on a test, quiz, study, or missing homework comes with the territory of education (most people). Mistakes will happen. I reflect, find the cause of the poor performance, and strive to do better the next time. I have to set sight on the task ahead and plan for the future. It takes away from progress if we are stuck in the past by worrying, catching up, and making up. Life then becomes more complicated to balance. We mustn't dwell on our mistakes. Dwelling allows for self-discontent, shame, and regret. We deal with a mistake by acknowledging it happened. See, that is a small fragment of your life. Understand that there is always a worse outcome. Take what information you can get from it and improve for next time.

Dealing With The Negative

There are always harmful components in your life. We have to take measures to prevent ourselves from being affected harshly. Life will often give warning signs. We have to contemplate the consequences in our decision-making. If you develop foresight, then you can better avoid the negative. We do not know the future, but we can anticipate it. Sometimes, we avoid the trouble as a whole. Plan ahead of time, evaluate, and act. There may be unforeseen consequences. We must be adaptive by maintaining an excellent internal state and calmness. The worst decisions come from panic, fear, and anger. The negative is unavoidable, but it all starts with controlling what is in the head. The philosopher Epictetus uses the bath example when dealing with the problems he foresaw. Sometimes, by expecting the negative to happen, the effects are weaker than when they do. It will aid in alleviating the intensity of an emotion from dire circumstances. I have an example of my own. Imagine you are walking into a nearby convenience store. One of the two products you are searching for is completely out. Upon searching, your foot stepped into a small spill that made your shoes sticky. You continue your search while listening to each step's sticky, peeling sound. Finally, you've accepted your loss and head to checkout. As you reach the register, you look up; boom! A senior citizen is playing his lottery numbers. Your simple three-minute store visit turned into ages. When going through any challenging time, remember that some bad things are bound to happen. We should expect some inconvenience to occur at times. Do not let it throw you into a state of turbulence. Do not always live thinking that something terrible will happen. Next, how you perceive something will determine the intensity of the impact on you. Our mind is a powerful filter for information. Changing your perception can help avoid undesirable emotions and negative attitudes. Some things are much harder to deal with than others. For instance, finding a ticket on your car, forgetting your morning coffee, stepping on a wet bathroom floor, or cranberry juice stain on your wedding dress. We can put our minds at ease by viewing those bad things as a lesson. Think to yourself, "Life is one big class I'm still learning from." In addition to perception, we must consider the level of importance of something or someone and how that influences our emotions. The more important something is to you, the greater its effect on you. For example, the death of a loved one is more impactful than the death of your roommate spider. This is not to say you should not hold your loved one near and dear to your heart. Awareness of what is essential to us allows us to take better control over ourselves emotionally. We can then shift our level of attachment. In the cases we can not prepare for and prevent, we need coping mechanisms to deal with the aftermath. Coping mechanisms are vital to dealing with hardship. Coping mechanisms include writing, painting, mechanics, long walks, martial arts, acting, eating healthy snacks, building, reading, dancing, sports, and engaging friends. I encourage you to search for your coping mechanisms. Make a coping mechanism bucket list. Avoid maladaptive coping mechanisms such as drinking, smoking, gambling, and drugs. None of those substances add to a healthier and happier life. They serve as distractions from progress and growth. Instead of tackling problems, people temporarily run away and get caught in a cycle of being troubled. Also, do not blame other people for issues in your life. In a sense, it takes away accountability, and therefore, it takes our minds away from working on improvement. It will take away your honesty.

Creating Meaning

When we think of meaning, we ponder a life worth waking up for. We want a life that has value and use. People receive meaning in a variety of ways. You must search for your passion and act on it to create meaning in your life. We all can develop our passion or come across it instantaneously. The search is on us individually, although others can guide us. Role models or teachers can give us tools or experiences to develop or act on our passion. Purpose can stem from many places. People get meaning from many other sources, such as community service, work, medicine, literature, acting, art, family, and martial arts. Time with family and friends could be a significant thing. We can create meaning in our day even when it is seemingly impossible. When you are working on a given task that may be seemingly pointless, find something in that work to improve upon. Create challenges like timing, achieving a high level of complexity, or competition with others. There is always an objective to improve or focus on. For entrepreneurs and businesspeople, this means they might assume building more effective products for consumers. There may be an aspiration to become more innovative, creative, and novel. Creating meaning in your life might mean promoting authenticity in life. That is to live day to day without a mask. Be yourself and let the world know who you are. My meaning in life comes from helping people reshape their minds to have less stress and solve problems. That is why I write books and love engaging in heartfelt discussions. My passion is to create a much more moral-based environment. Passion will take some effort to maintain. My passions require me to go through experiences and study. I learned that various philosophies, experiences, and creative thinking are stepping stones to fulfill my meaning and purpose. Having people benefit from reading what I write is one of the best feelings in the world. Martial arts also bring meaning to my life. I can teach and assist others to protect themselves. I can perform complex movements and techniques I never thought I'd do. I gain a better overall physique. On top of that, I supplement my physical development with moral education. I look forward to those things, so I wake up in the morning. What gives you meaning?

Seeking Help

Seeking help is something many people have an issue with. It may demonstrate vulnerability, weakness, pitifulness, and lack of control to some people. Seeking help is powerful because it allows you to improve an unwanted condition. Whether mentally, physically, or emotionally, seeking help is critical to becoming a good human being and making progress. Seeking help first requires knowing you have a problem.

Examine your life and reflect on what your problems may be. You will have to think outside the box as it could be more profound. It could help to compare the issue to something. By finding relationships between problems and aspects of life, we learn more. There could be a spiderweb of connected issues. On top of that, there is always cause and effect. Could my actions have brought bad outcomes? Is my mentality ruining relationships? Could my self-esteem be low? Is that why the environment feels uncomfortable? Ask yourself hard-hitting questions. Also, other people are great tools with which to find our issues. They can see what we miss. Sometimes, talking through the issue helps us reach realizations. When you identify the problem, go to those who have overcome the problem. Find those who may have answers for you to conquer your issue. Furthermore, assisting others can be an exciting task. When giving help, we must know ourselves to help others. We have to leave behind our issues. We also have to live in a way that validates our help. We have to reduce our prejudice and judgment. We can not help people when we are jealous, ill-disciplined, and maladaptive in our habits. When attempting to help people, you should not lend a hand to peel their fingers off a cliff. Moreover, people may have to be forced to get help. Sometimes, when people are thrown into the pits of assistance, they can learn to accept it and become vulnerable. Let them know what the help can do for them. Find their reason/s to improve themselves. Let them know what it can do for their children, relationships, finances, and purpose. Acknowledge what it can do for their career, business, or self-esteem. Stay positively and enthusiastically consistent in your pursuits. Motivate people by letting them know their positive aspects and uplifting critiques. Let the positive be twice as good as the bad. A great message I received from one of my mentors is sometimes you have to help them in a way they understand. That is to treat them according to what they are receptive to. We should help, but remember to avoid your detriment. There is a healthy boundary you should maintain regarding this. You could get pulled into the storm they are in. Sometimes, the Daoist approach works. Let things take their course. Some people have to go through harsh lessons. For some people, a bad experience may be enough. People may have to go through several events to reach a robust and critical point, make a difference, and seek help.

Advice

There are aspects of people's advice to consider. Watch who you receive advice from. Sometimes, people do not know enough to speak on a subject. Some people give their perspective according to their experience, which may not necessarily suit you. People can only offer you what they live and learn from others. We have to acknowledge people's limitations. If you want to walk a similar path, take their guidance and act on it. For example, in the context of money, do not take advice from people with bad money management. If you choose to write a book, go to the person succeeding. Take advice from the well-off in your desired destination, and you'll be closer to reaching that stage. Besides those who have succeeded, some people are trying and making progress. They can give insight on what to avoid and what works in the context of their experience. They are on a path to becoming great, and they are the ones to seek knowledge from as well. When you want to reach a certain level or status, take advice from those already there. Information is more available than ever. Information is the key to domination. A book, video, or podcast can be our education. The wrong information is the key to doom. Some people want you to fail. They may not be content with their own lives. Their advice will steer you away from greatness and prosperity, strip your goals, and belittle your achievements. They see the negative in the heavens and the positive in hell. Do not take advice from these people because they'll try to discourage you. Use your intuition to discern the good and bad people. When you are interacting with anyone, listen to that gut feeling. Life is short, and the days go by faster as you age, so you do not want to be derailed. The advisors will come, and the good people will mean well. These people want you to win. They want you to make shifts in your life for the better. When receiving advice, specific questions are relevant. Get as much information as you can muster.

Materialism

From a young age, I learned that obtaining the latest games, toys, cars, and jewelry was important to some people. There was a need to show off and get attention. Materialism brings status to some people. It was also a display of wealth. The desire to receive compliments and acknowledgments was evident. As I grew older, some things did not change. Most people idolize those who display wealth and status through materials. Some problems follow materialistic desires and idolization. When people long for objects they can not obtain, they become disappointed and have lower self-worth.

Materialism can lead to sadness. They may go to great lengths to get what they want to their detriment. People can become arrogant and boastful when they get the objects they need. Materialism can lead to people becoming too prideful. These people often look down on and speak negatively about others. People lose money trying to keep up by gaining and maintaining what they desire. Materialism brings a loss to net worth. People become stressed trying to outdo others. Materialism can lead people to be competitive. People will increase their distractions and reduce the prioritization of what matters. (Prioritize progress, societal issues, family, self-development, etc.) Showing off wealth or gain brings jealousy and envy. Materialism can put a target on your back and develop enemies. As I reflect on life, I learned something. I learned early that what I once held dear was eventually no longer a thought. Think of your possessions like the toys you desired and favored as a child. You no longer want those old toys anymore. Once you have had the object and decided you've received all you can from it, it loses its importance to you. As time passes and you reflect on your desires, you may laugh at how silly it was. This is because the direction of what you find important has changed. It may help to think that we own nothing outside our bodies and minds. At some point, even those will be out of our control. Also, materialism can ruin relationships. Relationships are ruined when others' materialism can create hierarchy of who has and has not their desires. We can lose friends and family trying to maintain materialistic status. It can lead us to see others as commodities and transactions for gain. Materialism can make people seek profit over connection in our relationships. People place material possessions above others, thus ruining relationships.

Objects

You see gold on earth,
I see the beauty on earth,
We are both at odds.

Don't Stop

There are two paths in life: the easy road and the road called "what I know I should do." One of the biggest deterrents to progress is favoring comfortability. Following what we know we should is a tall order. At times, it is like a mountain, the perceivably immovable. It is a challenging but fruitful road. As we move to the fruit, we need tools to keep us going. Two difficulties of climbing the top of the mountain are maintaining your persistence and motivation. To support both, we ought to find an honest person to keep us focused. Find some meaning through the path you are taking. Find a weakness to improve upon; what you enjoy in something you perceive unenjoyable. We have to keep our desired destination constantly in mind. Avoid the people who discourage you from your process. Be reasonable with all of your goals. Avoid those who throw down your thoughts and propose something less. Enthusiasm for the work is also important. In the process, find what's fun and interesting. Remember, on our climb up to the top of the mountain, we fall off the cliff when we give up. When we give up on tasks, we teach ourselves the habit of quitting. To give up is to be free of worry, obligation, hard work, and discomfort. I encourage you to not give up on the process. Keep in mind what giving up will bring. Contemplate your potential regret as time passes. Your potential will vanish, and unknown doors will remain closed. Also, you may begin to limit your aspirations and capabilities with other objectives. Your motivation and inspiration will self-destruct. You become content with achieving minimal and bearing little fruit. Keep your mind on the consequences you desire. As a side note, parents should encourage and push their children whenever they are struggling. Teach them to follow through. Tell them to run through the finish line. Tell them that most objectives are achievable. Whatever is doable can be done. Encourage them to make their weak points strong. Position them to explore their talents and make them stronger.

Focused

Staying on top of your mission is a hard thing to do. There are always external and internal factors that influence your attention. While on our mission, we must find something that will hold our attention and engage our minds to the point where we lose that concept of time. For example, when I talked to my philosophy professor after class, I enjoyed the conversation. It was a fun, intellectual dialogue bouncing ideas back and forth. It brought different insights and ways of thinking. We lost the concept of time through our conversation. Thirty minutes passed, but we weren't concerned about anything but the topic. What is that thing that will put you in a space to be in the moment? A space where nothing else matters. The benefit to this is worry goes away for a short time. It helps you become relaxed. You can perform much more effectively. We need our environmental conditions to be aligned with our focus. We need to find the space to be most attentive to our objective. When I have to do schoolwork, I prefer to be in a secluded space on campus. It was just the space that put my mind into a particular mode for proper focus. When practicing my martial arts, I find it easier to focus at the dojang (training facility). Where is your place for making progress? Aside from location, how do you manipulate the environment to suit your focus? Some might benefit from lighting a scented candle, switching colored lights, or turning on a waterfall. In addition, I think that to maintain focus on a mission, we have to love it. We can complete anything by producing a deep bond and desire to make it happen.

Be Persistent

Persistence is needed to meet your goals and milestones. We have to be obsessed with completing a task. We have to press on through troubles, grief, and mistakes. Before I began college, I decided to write a book. I already had a chunk of the book started. I was working on my long-term project on my own time. I intended to finish the book by the time I graduated (slightly before or after). When college started, I had to put off my craft temporarily. I had to focus on grades first, and the problematic classwork reminded me that grades came first. When I had free time, I put my efforts towards the book. I worked on the book during fall, winter, spring, and summer breaks. I often use it for the book when I have time for leisure. I took time out to produce more free-verse poems and haiku. I had a "writing about literature" class in college. One area of the course included spoken word. When I created and displayed them, I saw that people liked it. I decided to put them in the book. In this way, I used my time in other areas of life to support my goal. I unintentionally came across something that I intentionally used to meet my goal. Another example of this was when I attended a fatherhood conference. I participated in the panel discussion on how men can improve. I brought up a story that turned out to be impactful, and it resonated with some. I used my memory to recall short stories to give life lessons. Moreover, I used my connections to create illustrations that make poetry come to life. I networked to find someone to help me materialize my vision. When the opportunity presented itself, I used my connections to publish my second book. The connections and networking allowed me to maintain my persistence. I was not stalled or slowed down. There was always an opportunity to do more and get closer to my goal. As opportunities came, I took them. This is key because those four years of college were rough. During those four years, I dealt with criticism. Some people had ill intentions toward me. I ignored the bad and used philosophy to build my resilience. A few times, I had financial worries regarding school. I worked a ton of hours, but I've had fortunate opportunities. My second time dealing with death might have been the worst. It was my second-semester junior year. I did not dwell in grief. I coped with exercise, discussing grief, and writing. This prevented me from staying in a bad state and maintaining focus. When hardship comes, find the mantra, be resilient, and seek help. Find it within yourself to overcome the issues and continue your pursuit. Furthermore, we are never too busy. You are never too busy for opportunity. The time for leisure could be time to make progress instead of parties and games. By the time I graduated, my persistence paid off. I completed my masterpiece slightly after I graduated in June 2022.

Martial Arts

The world is dangerous, so we must become hazardous, too. I always took a liking to martial arts. I loved watching movies, YouTube videos, and TV shows showing unique movements. Television and media inspired me to start my martial arts journey. My martial arts education began with my grandfather; we practiced Isshinryu. Isshinryu is one of the many karate styles practiced today. I would hang out with him over the summer in my teen years. After some time, I decided to move on to another martial art called ITF Taekwondo (International Taekwondo Federation). It is a traditional Korean martial art created by the founder, General Choi. ITF Taekwondo has helped me in several ways. A proper martial arts education with real-world application will enable you to defend and attack to keep yourself safe. It will help us develop morality and live to be an exceptional role model. Martial arts aid us in building confidence and improving our health, physique, and more. I want to emphasize good health because I lose all I have faster if I am not in good health. Within the martial arts world, when you improve your physical body, the more you improve your safety and longevity. I think that martial arts will help people overcome their thoughts and limitations. Within training, you are motivated to move your body in a way you did not know you could. You expand the parameters of what you thought was possible to do. When we learn our capabilities, we become much more confident in ourselves. We gain the confidence to set higher goals. For many martial artists, there's no need to fight at all. Through confidence and high self-esteem, we do not resort to violence against others. There is no need to prove oneself or one's manhood. Self-defense is getting away and seeking help. Self-defense is de-escalating and fighting when needed. Self-defense is being alive and unharmed. In addition, martial arts have many more benefits. It is therapeutic because we escape the ills of the world around us. We can put ourselves in flow and help train our focus. On top of that, you will have the chance to increase your social capital and meet new people from all sorts of backgrounds. Martial arts also has a way of humbling you. It reminds you that you must continuously improve, especially when outclassed. It helps us remember that someone is always better than you at something. You learn that there is always someone much more competent. You will make mistakes, but there will always be mistakes. All we can do is improve and avoid repeating mistakes. Martial arts teaches us that mistakes are okay and allow us to help others overcome challenges. You may embarrass yourself, be fearful, and be nervous, but it is worth it for growth. Another aspect of martial arts is the moral components. In ITF Taekwondo, we have the five tenets for guidance while we practice the art. The five tenets are courtesy, integrity, perseverance, self-control, and indomitable spirit. Other martial arts have their moral guidelines. These are some qualities and habits we can form to live a good life. I encourage you to develop your tenets to life. What ethical guidelines do you place for yourself? Treat this like the vision board, five-year plan, and wall of achievements. My five tenets are being teachable, kindness, persistence, discipline, and courage.

Open Mind

An open mind is much more free, critical, and knowledgeable. Through my schooling, I had to engage with four different attributes to help me become a better, well-rounded person. The first attribute was global awareness. Global awareness examines the life, realities, and circumstances of people outside of North America. The global awareness attribute strives to break the ignorance about historical and current events, figures, and places. Furthermore, the college requires the second attribute of diversity, which focuses on people's and cultural differences—both combat negative preconceived notions and critical judgments. We learn about people's way of life and the causes and effects of their conditions today. Often, in class discussions, we speak on potential solutions to diversity issues. I observed people overcome their judgments and presuppositions. With diversity education, we can throw away our ignorant ways of thinking about others, working with others becomes easier, and we become more understanding. I have an example of this in my first english class freshman year. The class was centered around discussing differences in people's political outlook. Each of us wrote about an individual of our choice. After writing, we would review each other's writing and give feedback. The person I reviewed wrote about Colin Kaepernick kneeling during the American national anthem. The Student disliked Kaepernick because kneeling during the national anthem is presumed to be disrespectful. In response to his writing, I talked about Kaepernick's civil rights connection to kneeling during the American national anthem. He kneeled because of the injustice (police brutality/killings) within the country, which contradicts the anthem itself. Through an open mind, someone who once saw disgrace in kneeling now views it as noble. As a result, people can look beyond the actions of individuals to focus on systems. Moreover, the third attribute is justice, which provides what right and wrong is in the light of politics, morality, ethics, law, etc. We learn about the ailments of society plenty, but we are learning tools to deal with injustice. Some examples of tools include parrhesia, argumentation, research, data management, film, and more. Finally, the fourth attribute, ethics, provides moral guidelines we can implement in our own lives. Examples of ethical concepts are deontology, Confucianism, Ubuntu, Animal, and virtue ethics. These components help us develop our way of approaching the problems we encounter. They help us set the tone for our relationship with the community. These four attributes helped me develop a better social and moral standpoint. It also assisted my open-mindedness to blossom. I grew a better understanding of others and their condition. I encourage our children to learn these four attributes continuously. We should also sharpen our strength in those areas. Education will keep us grounded, humble, and grateful. It will help us maintain relatability and think more critically about our condition. Acknowledge the truth and do not sugarcoat it. Learn all you can and embrace humanity so that we grow. The wise have an open mind. The wise are accepting and almost all-embracing.

Change

Change is a good thing because it allows everything to become better. At times, change is a hard thing to accept. It is tough to accept when we do not believe there is something to change. As people, we can stagnate our thinking, values, behaviors, etc. Be able to adapt and avoid rigid states of being. We all have things we can improve. We change not for others but for our own sake. Build the vocabulary and get rid of vulgarity. Get off the lazy road; ride the wave of your progress. Get away from entertainment and move towards learning. It is imperative we evolve. What is now does not always have to be. Some people think they are above change as if a higher form of themselves could not happen. That way of thinking is immature. Perfection is something no one has seen before. Self-improvement is a continuous process. Improvement could be in any area, such as patience, agility, physique, financial literacy, or speaking. The person you are today is not forever. Change is a lifelong but fruitful journey. We change by changing our habits. We can subtract, substitute, or add to our daily routine. We have to educate ourselves to develop mental shifts to change.

Advocacy

The need for advocacy is more significant when people view circumstances as unchangeable. These people need a change of thinking. They put little to no effort into improving unfavorable conditions. These people bring acceptance to the negative and teach satisfaction for generations to come. We also can not be content with current conditions when better is possible. We can not be satisfied with the superficial progress (flashy advancements). If the major issues aren't being reduced, then there is no progress. Some people desire to change and act upon their visions of brighter futures. Over time, we have seen people change individuals and people massively. Through advocacy, so much has changed, like policy and education programs, but there is more to do. Engaging in advocacy is doing your part to improve the community, the people nearest to you, and yourself. Turning away from advocacy is like neglecting others and, therefore, yourself. Other people shape us. Neglect is a slow-moving poison affecting people around you, even those born after you. The power of advocacy is in setting conditions so that the community has more opportunities to thrive. Our environment has a powerful influence on us. Our community influences our pockets, fear, safety, emotional well-being, perspective, and resources. Advocacy is another topic that should be placed within the school system. We receive education but sometimes fail to teach its application. What good is any tool if you have yet to learn how or what to use it for? We are given intellectual tools that often go to waste. These tools are writing, statistics, public speaking, argumentation, and law. Lastly, remember, activism is to be done from a place of need, not to receive fame or exposure. It is not something done temporarily out of boredom. Take part in advocacy in any way. For change to come, advocacy is

necessary to reach community needs, and we have
to engage in it.

Criticism

One of the learning objectives in college is
to send a proper email. It is required to maintain
professional standards. I was in a rush one day to
email my professor. I told the professor I was sick
and would not attend class. I was dealing with
COVID-19 about a few days before classes started.
He told me I could receive a Zoom invitation for
Monday's class. The following sentence said, "In
the meantime, you can work on sending an email in
proper format." Some people would consider that
rude or slight. Some may think they should retaliate
in a passive-aggressive fashion. When I read it, I
was taken aback. I thought about it for a second. I
replied, "Thank you for your email and
consideration. Have a great weekend." (in proper
format). I did not intend for that to be sarcastic or
passive-aggressive. I meant that message genuinely.
In my mind, his email registered to me as kind,

considerate, and caring. I knew how to send a proper email, and he knew I knew how to send an appropriate email. I did not care enough and neglected it. He was gracious enough to remind me to care. He helped me see my mistake and went the extra mile to inform me. I went the extra mile to send a proper email after that. When receiving criticism, think first that there is something you may want to change. I do not see it as an attack but as a helping hand. In my case, I maintained professionalism in my email. We all have our faults, although we do not always have people around us to help lift us when we fall. Sometimes, they help lift us out of a hole we sometimes unconsciously fall into. Think of criticism as a tool. Be mindful that criticism can come from the tongue of hate, dislike, jealousy, and so on. It varies depending on the context, so learn the difference. No matter the criticism, how things are said is just as important as what was said. I have thick skin, and you should develop or refine it. How you think about it will influence how you feel about it. Change the way you think.

Distractions

Distractions are the bane of our existence. At the same time, it can keep our boat afloat amid a storm. Some examples are video games, TV, social media, alcohol, sports, and an ever-growing distraction, gambling. Distractions are the things that take us off task and off focus. They are the devil on our shoulders that tells us to take steps away from our goals. He tells us to get off the stairway of progress. I was much more guilty of the TV and video games at a younger age. As I aged and increased maturity, I developed a balance. Eventually, I decided to prioritize growth. When I chose to cut my bad distractions, I made progress. I shifted the bad distractions into learning, motivating, and experimenting. I would do research and watch educational and motivational videos. I instilled within myself a drive to become greater. I applied my focus to other things that brought me growth. In this way, distractions can be a great thing. Healthy distractions are what we need. It wouldn't hurt to read a book and escape our world. Long walks can help us gather our thoughts and contemplate. A good comedy special will take the world away. It will help you get away from the troubles of life temporarily. Appropriate distractions can be like a recharge for us, but we need to be frugal with our distractions. Too much distraction can guide us to neglect the road to progress. Making our goal a distraction is a solid mental change that will benefit us. We become more productive when we take our downtime away from distractions and put it towards our mission. Whatever you're working on, let that be something to relax yourself. My distraction became my book and learning about business. Typing my book was much more engaging and enjoyable than a paper on something I did not care about. Change your distraction, and if your mission is work, then let your distraction be healthy and productive.

Communication

I attended fatherhood classes to learn about what it means to be a dad. I wanted to learn how to be a good and effective one. Communication was one of the topics we covered. Communication is a hard thing to do sometimes. There were complaints whenever I had a conversation with my significant other about the day. The complaints were mostly about work. Before the communication class, I preferred not to listen to my partner because I did not want to absorb the negative. I did not want to hear about her troubles, which caused friction between her and me. One day, the friction changed. On the day of the communication class, I changed my thinking about communication in my relationship. This shift in thinking came to me when I listened to other men talk about their experiences. There were many small lessons I learned. One lesson I learned was that she found me important enough to talk to about her problems. She felt secure enough to discuss her feelings, concerns, and troubles. I also had to improve my display of attention to the conversation. When being talked to, keeping eye contact, using body-to-body direction, and having no distractions is key. Having intimate engagement without cell phones, television, and so on is critical. Even if I heard everything, she did not feel heard if I was not visibly attentive. Further on in the session, I learned to listen without blurting a word. It's rude when we interrupt a talking point. It also tells the person talking that we are not valuing what they say. I concluded that I needed to ask before I gave input. Examples of this include: May I offer advice? Can I provide a solution? We have to have rules within communication. We need parameters to maintain healthy, attentive, and productive communication. You should establish rules like no profanity, one person talking at a time, and not assuming or dismissing how each other feels. Besides setting rules, body language was another topic we covered. Read each other to learn sensitive or cheerful areas. Observe leg activity, folded arms, hands, and posture. Behavior is relevant to any conversation. The ability to feel out the direction of conversation is key. When it comes to issues in a conversation, I've discovered not to make the person the problem. Attack the issue and not the person. When there is screaming, for instance, address the loud noise instead of the significant other. Understanding the other person is imperative to maintain good communication. Clarity is needed in all cases. Besides our relationships, we talked about reprimanding children. During the conversation, I remembered an exercise I learned from ITF taekwondo. When I evaluated kids during a belt test, I was instructed to give one positive and one negative critique. The positive and negative method balances out the performer's feelings about their experience. The method will prevent the kid from thinking I can do no wrong. It also prevents the kid from thinking everything I do is terrible. It encourages a focus on positive outcomes while acknowledging that the mistakes need change. If we give them a heavy negative response, the students become discouraged from continuing the art. Children who receive heavy adverse reactions can be dragged into poor self-worth, emotional challenges, and more negative behavior. Their focus is what their mind is directed to. We need to add a positive element to reassure them they are not lacking. After giving specific critiques, we practice how to perform so weaknesses become strengths. We are to maintain a calm or enthusiastic voice. We provide attentive posture with smiles. We set the tone for the environment so that people are motivated. Good expressions also allow people to become comfortable around us. The students are likely to come to us about issues they have down the line. Lastly, I attended a healing circle certification class. We must end on a good or neutral note when closing the circles. It is complimented with a breathing exercise to center ourselves. During the circles, we talk about a lot of tough subjects. To avoid being caged by the destructive emotions that may arise, we have to close with a good outlook. When we discuss anything with anyone, it is beneficial to maintain a good closing and leave on a happy note. Confidentiality is also a component of the circle, and the most important one is that these lessons apply to young and old.

Reflection

Reflection is one of the most powerful and simple tools we have. Walking down the roads of our passion, progress, possibilities, positivity, and success is imperative. We also must trudge through the trail of our jealousy, anguish, grievance, fears, and pests. Reflection can be a hard thing to do, but it gives us clarity about our circumstances. The more detailed and honest you are in your thoughts, the better the mental mirror you craft for yourself. This mirror is soul-moving and eye-watering. Reflect on what others say of you from a genuine place. Reminder: people can teach us a lot about ourselves. This process makes people much more aware of what needs to change and improve. Awareness is the first step to creating change and improvement. Then, we have to put things into action so that both happen. Another remarkable aspect of reflection is that we remember lessons and stories that put things into perspective. With reflection, you get the lesson's more profound meaning and complexity. You'll grow wiser and more mature because you'll take your learning deeper. Your mind will go from the water's surface to the deep, unknown sea others are afraid to enter. It is scary, yet beautiful. Reflection is taking a class. As we experience more in life, the more we get out of that repetitive class. It is a never-ending education. I recommend we write down all those things that trouble us. Title this the self-improvement bucket list. Every day, we will work on crossing off those negative things that prevent us from becoming great people. The catch is we will continuously add on to this list. Some things might make the list so long it will fade! The greatest challenge we must conquer is our comfort with what is on the list. We get comfortable because we lack something. My great-grandmother used to call that something grit. Grit is perseverance, persistence, working smart, and being efficient. The

grit needed to get what you have to get done, done.
Reflect often and reflect deeply.

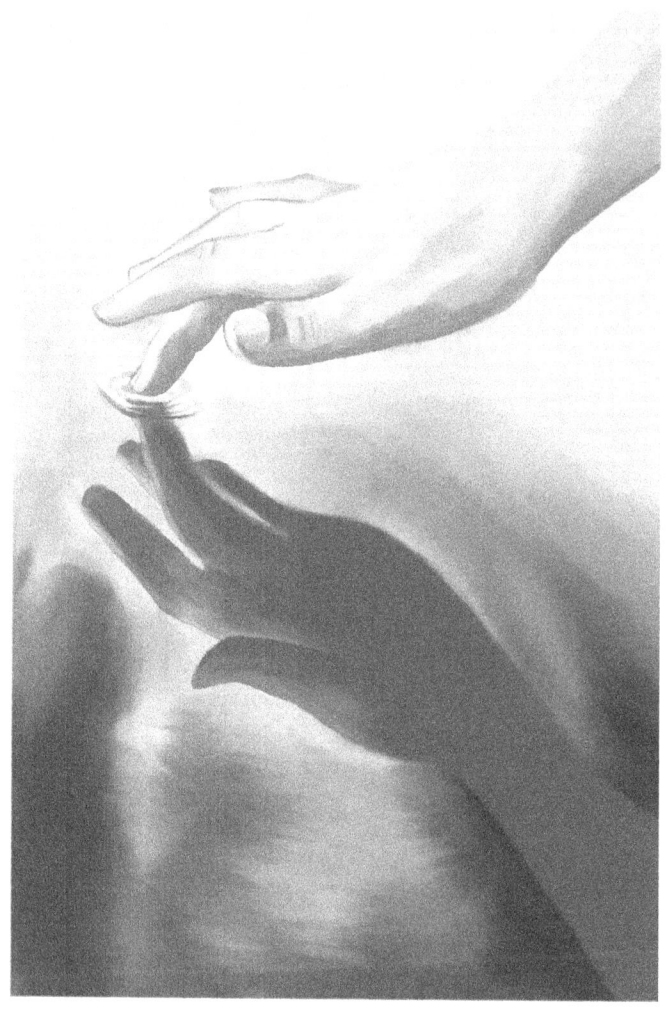

Vulnerability

I met with one of my doctor friends to give him my book. He was impressed, and I was happy he loved it. We discussed each other's book processes and gave advice. One of the subjects that came up during our conversation was vulnerability. There is a power to being vulnerable. Vulnerability is the exposure of your heart. Vulnerability is the release of all the dirt and trauma from our past. To some, it is the equivalent of self-harm. In my experience, I am less likely to be hurt when I allow myself to become vulnerable. To be vulnerable is a process of confronting our troubles. If we do it enough, it is like becoming desensitized. When you are vulnerable to others, opinions and judgments aren't as important. You would have fought through your trouble well enough to share your heart. When you do this, your days are happier, and your burden is lighter. You choose what will affect you. Reaching happiness is a task. If we discuss the things that trouble us, we get closer to delight. By confronting our troubles, we get much closer to joy.

Moreover, find your way of expression. We have many ways to find relief through the expression of music, art, clothing, tattoos, jewelry, and religious practice. This way, we can gradually grow closer to vulnerability and build thick skin about our experiences. We can do a magnificent deed for the world when we show our hearts. Billions of people on Earth have shared experiences similar to yours. Your vulnerability can help others get through a tough time. By the courage you have mustered, you've given others the bravery to overcome their trouble. You triggered someone to look at things a different way. You prevented someone from doing horrible things to themselves and others. We all take part in the progress of the world. By being vulnerable, we can make the world a better place. In my first personal book, I exposed the trouble and fears I had as a youth in education and relationships. That book was a way of release. We must find our way of release and make some money from it. When people do not release, express, or allow vulnerability in some form, it can eat at us. We live a life of more emotional and mental pain than necessary. Do not live with the burden you don't have to bear.

Peeled Skin

I saw others' spirits exposed when they spoke.

While listening I contemplated,

I thought about how weak I might have been,

Later I grew strength when I found my talent.

I started to shave my skin off little by little.

The more came off the cooler the atmosphere got.

Later, the skin became resilient.

Impenetrable, this is part of progressing to perfection.

I think of this as part of my purpose and profession.

Forgiveness

Forgiveness means to stop holding a grudge or resentment against an offender. To hold resentment is to have anger or distaste towards something that has done us wrong. Forgiveness is powerful, but reaching it can be a big step. There is a mental shift you have to make. The mental shift is no longer allowing the wrong done to you to affect you. Think of the wrong done to you as wrong done to them. They became worse human beings. The wrongdoers did not improve themselves from it. They did not improve, but you have a chance to. Think of yourself as superior to those who do wrong to you. Do not let anger strip gold from your inner being. Do not drop to their level utilizing revenge. Another thing that helps to reach forgiveness is understanding the other person's side of things. Obtaining this understanding does not mean the wrong done is acceptable. Understanding puts ourselves in the minds of others so that we can be more agreeable. It will educate us about the other person's condition, circumstances, and issues. We only see perspectives from our point of view. That is a limitation to growth in some ways, so we have to get into another way of thinking. We come to understand why they did what they did. This puts our mind at ease. Another way I can conceive of reaching forgiveness is through distance and

alternative focus. Get away from the wrongdoers
and apply attention to what will advance you. Allow
yourself to be preoccupied with progress. Moreover,
find someone sensible to talk to so that you can
successfully forgive. Someone with more
experience in forgiving someone else can help you
go a long way. Not everything is easy to forgive, but
it is not impossible.

Accountability Partner

My most memorable accountability partner
was a great man I encountered through the college
experience. He is an elder from one of the diversity
offices at my college. We talked about the casual
and general college stuff when I met him. What is
your major and minor if you have it? What are you
planning to do with it? Outside of that, we would
have other conversations about our likes, such as
poetry and community involvement. He would
always ask what was up. Like most of us, I give a
good and neutral answer. We want to hear the praise
and positive feedback. His "what's up" is ambiguous

because it's looking for the good and the bad. I liked that he addressed both sides. If you offer only the good to the accountability partner, then you are not being accountable to people who mean well by offering advice and criticism. Accountability partners often see what we can not. They bring clarity and knock us back into reality. When my grades were low, my partner would help me find the root of the problem. We looked at the things within and outside of myself that needed to be changed for growth. He knew I could do better when I did poorly. He expected nothing but the highest from me. Each time I visited him, I made an effort to return to him with some progress. I didn't particularly appreciate coming empty-handed. I wouldn't say I liked returning with bad news, but I gave that too. An external accountability partner assists with maintaining the internal partner. The first and most crucial accountability partner is in the mirror. How honest are you with yourself? Can you be honest without sugarcoating your growth and faults?

Elements Of Influence

Many elements influence society. I want to highlight the narratives. Narratives are one of the significant components that impact people. Narratives are stories we develop about ourselves and what others develop about us. Narratives are created every second of the day, depending on how we walk, blink, and talk—everything we do matters in our lives and relation to others because it creates a narrative. Our actions, thoughts, and behaviors should conform to positive narrative building. An example of positive narrative building comes from my travels. College requires copious amounts of reading. I developed a healthy habit of carrying and reading a book when I have time to wait. Whether on a train, bus, or waiting room, I carried a book. I needed to read a ton for my schooling. I even had a pen with a highlighter to ensure I marked and absorbed what I read. It inadvertently helped shape a narrative about me and the people alike. Most people look on with generally curious, contemplative looks and, at times, a look of admiration. Conversations were even sparked from it. People would ask what I am reading and learn more about me. I shape narratives online as well. Even on social media, I always aim to show myself in a productive, motivational, and inspirational manner. I host podcasts for an organization I'm with. I enjoy interviewing and connecting with people in business and entrepreneurs. These people further reshape the narrative around capabilities and thoughts about people like me. What can you do to change your narrative and the narrative of the people alike? Taking control of our narrative is relevant because it shapes how we see ourselves and how others look at us. The narratives affect the opportunities, resources, relationships, and other social aspects of our lives. While developing a narrative, be critical of the one shown to you. Not all stories show people in a positive light. Good stories are often untold and replaced by bad ones for views or popularity. The danger of taking on false, negative narratives is that it shapes the persistence of generalizations, prejudgement, and discrimination. Famous and political people are essential to watch out for. They impact us through their ideas, perspectives, what they sign, narratives, etc. Our brain is a sponge that soaks up what others do or say in the spotlight. It is significant to discern honesty, ethics, and morals. Some people do not have the most excellent intentions and the most productive outlook. We have to ensure people follow their advice. Not everyone will do what they talk about. Taking a wrong or delusional perspective can pave the road to unintentional self-punishment, self-hate, or a terrible outlook on others. People must learn, develop their minds, and think for themselves. The most dangerous people or entities are sometimes the heaviest tools for pushing harmful narratives. They excel at influencing behavior and thought. Given the weight of media messages, searching for the truth is even more critical than ever. Sometimes, we must cut the chains linking popular opinion and our minds. We have to keep our mental fortitude strong. By doing this, we avoid regurgitating unproductive ways of thinking. There are many influences to narratives we have to watch out for. Music and television might be the biggest. We have to absorb progressive and healthy thinking, not what is detrimental. Take control of your story.

Self-Sufficiency

Self-sufficiency is very relevant to progression. Self-sufficiency forces us to adapt and gain a better perspective to move farther. Learning how to fish in the context of self-sufficiency is needed. When you know how to fish, you no longer have to rely on others to get you what you need. My mentor, who published the first book I co-authored, assisted me with publishing my second personal book. She taught me the process of producing the book. She helped me by providing the resources to realize my vision. I now know what it takes to create a book and can do it independently. I do not have to rely on someone as I once did. I am continuously grateful for her. Find this person in any prospective field that will teach you how to fish. When the opportunity comes, take it willingly, but be cautious. Act on your talents and gifts to pave the way. Fishing has many benefits. Fishing helps us make money and save money. By learning to cook, one is comfortable buying groceries to cook with. Cooking at home is better for your health and your pockets, and you have control. If you cook well and safely, people can buy your food. When we eat out for convenience, the food is most likely unhealthy; we have little control over its contents, and we lose more money. In this case, when we go to a fast food place, we rely on other people much more. Relying on others intensely can become a detriment to you. Self-sufficient people need to be watched. They are go-getters and use time more effectively. Time is well-spent on productivity. These people are finishers; they attack their obstacles head-on. They are actively seeking help, researching, building, networking, etc. These people have the best use of the time allowed on Earth.

Discipline

Discipline is one of the essentials for maintaining growth. Without discipline, life can fall apart. My great-grandmother probably had one of the greatest discipline methods. She constantly gave me lessons about moral and ethical concepts. Besides my great-grandmother, I received discipline from my elders through the programs I was involved in. They gave their wisdom and thoughts on what can make life good. They also serve as an example of behaving in a public setting. They taught us how to manage our emotions, treat a young lady and family, maintain health, and principles around personal pursuits. They gave advice and laid out their path. The advice lays a potential blueprint for avoiding what leads us to the gutter. I benefited from the knowledge of how to carry myself and how to deal with my emotions appropriately. They taught me there are higher objectives to strive for and how to stay on track. As time passed, I joined the martial arts realm; it added to my discipline. We are to greet everyone with a bow or shake by the arm. We are taught the respect of "yes, sir" and "yes, ma'am" when a command is given. Before a command, we are to say Mr. So and so or Miss/Mrs. So and so. We are reprimanded with physical exercises like push-ups when we respond inappropriately or not at all. In all standing cases, we are directed to stand straight with our hands held to our front or back, never at our sides. When we line up, it is by rank and age. In this way, I learn the discipline of being orderly and presentable. Lastly, discipline is abundant in what we can read. I think the most significant part of your discipline is the kind of philosophy you hold to yourself. Philosophy is fantastic for this topic, especially stoicism. Information is essential to everything from balancing diet, managing anger, and shaping your wealth. The more we know, the better off we will be. I was always taught to learn all that I could.

Legacy

Legacy is one of the most important considerations for our descendants. My great-grandmother gave me one of the most valuable things human beings could provide: time. What she did with the time is more important than time itself. She talked to me to instill guidance every time! She would talk my ears off for hours. I used to sit, listen, and absorb like a sponge at a young age. We sat until our last conversation, and I listened as if time never passed. I live on with her thoughts and memories that guide me when difficulty comes. As I grew, I developed my wisdom about the world through my learning and experiences. It is good to follow your thoughts. We must educate our family members about health risks, horrors, and the world's beauty. One of the issues I observed for many people is that certain information is shielded or blocked off. Ignorance often does more harm than knowing. Pass on how to deal with life and the lives around us. Moreover, reputation through narrative has an impact on descendants. Your family holds a reputation like everyone else, individually or collectively. Reputation can shape your image and, therefore, opportunity. Teaching your young ones their words, behaviors, and actions matter. Next, when we think of legacy, we often think of material things and monetary legacy. This includes life insurance, property, debt, land, savings, business, patents, products, and investments. Live life so that your descendants can thrive. This requires us to think about the future. We need descendants equipped with the means to do more and achieve more incredible than you did. Set conditions for your children to do well, help them pursue their desires, and maintain financial stability. Help them seek their talents or gifts; help them monetize it. Lastly, produce a legacy that will break down generational troubles. These troubles are in one's approach to thinking about relationships, aspirations, reputation, and finances. It's best to die with the descendants having fewer unnecessary problems. There will always be issues, but heal yourself as best you can.

About The Author

Dorian Scott Withrow Jr. was born on April 13th, 2000, in Buffalo, New York. His education was primarily through the Amherst Central School District. Dorian began his blossoming in high school by facing and conquering many challenges. His achievements were within many programs he

was involved in; programs such as Youth of the
Year, Jack and Jill of America, Leadership Buffalo,
and Breaking Barriers. He was accepted into
Canisius College in 2018, majored in Animal
Behavior Ecology and Conservation (ABEC), with
a minor in Philosophy. Throughout college, Dorian
was still involved in Breaking Barriers attending
meetings, participating in activism, and doing
podcasts. He was also involved in his newly found
passion, ITF Taekwondo. Dorian graduated from
Canisius College in May 2022.

Youth of the Year (Boys and Girls Club)

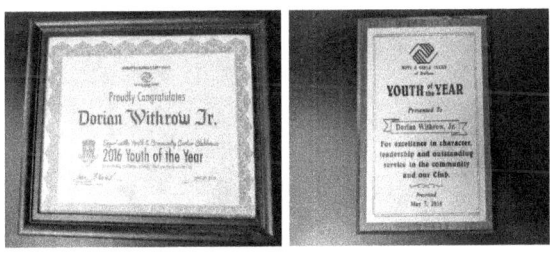

Youth of the Year is an achievement that youth in
Boys and Girls clubs accomplish for community
involvement, leadership, character, and even
mentorship for younger people. People who receive

this honor not only receive recognition, but have the opportunity to move on to greater milestones. Youth members selected from different Boys and Girls Clubs around the city are offered to take part in different workshops to meet the next stage. These workshops include public speaking, writing, teaching, etc. He did not meet the next stage, but out of six competitors, he came in second.

Jack & Jill Of America

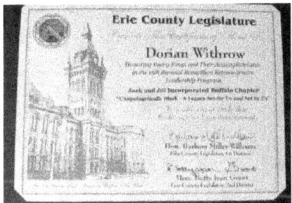 

Dorian was also involved in Jack & Jill of America, a program for young black males. The program held many workshops such as leadership, fitness, dress to impress, public speaking, and dance (West African and Urban Ballroom). This program allowed for the creation of a network among its members. Community service was another element of the program to instill the importance of serving exposure to many unique people and aided Dorian in character development. At the end of the program, boys become men through African rights of passage. The final ceremony involved our speeches, dance, and rights of passage. The boys got to give themselves a name when they became men. Dorian became Adwin (thinker and artist).

Leadership Buffalo

Leadership Buffalo was a program Dorian experienced during his first retreat. He met a lot of interesting people from special backgrounds. Leadership Buffalo also held a lot of workshops regarding leadership, cooking, dining etiquette (Lesson from a former butler of the queen of England), diversity, inclusion, and more. There was an amazing opportunity for teamwork and building more connections.

Honors and Rewards

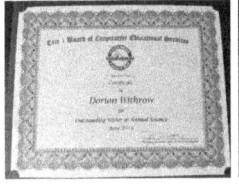 

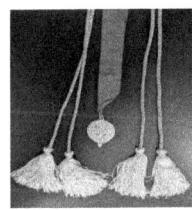 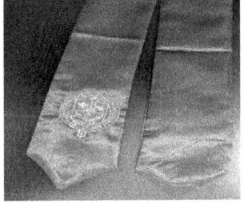

Dorian received many honors and rewards in high school. Dorian obtained the national honors society for maintaining merit roll in high school. He also attended Harkness Erie One Boces for Animal Science and earned national technical honor society. Dorian gained scholarships from Buffalo Urban League and Delta Sigma Theta Sorority. Finally, he graduated from high school in 2018 and pursued a bachelor's at Canisius College. As of now, he is a Canisius alumnus with a Bachelor of Science. Dorian had a strong liking for philosophy. His love for philosophy has led him to earn a place in Phi Sigma Tau, a Philosophical honor society, and be rewarded with the St. Thomas Aquinas Award in Philosophy for having demonstrated exceptional achievement in philosophy. Lastly, he was granted the Martin Luther King Award for promoting social justice, social harmony, civil rights, human rights, advocacy of the poor, and non-violence.

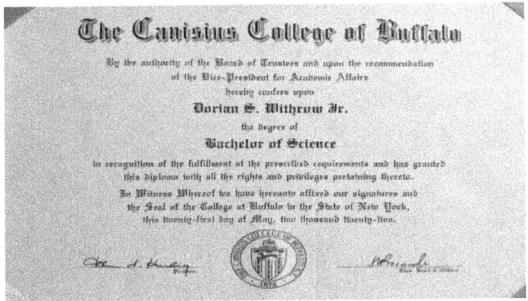

Dorian is a graduate and still a youth council
member of Breaking Barriers, a program in which
males of color ages twelve to twenty-four, act on

policy, mentoring, leadership, and improving work opportunities and conditions of other young people in education (just to name a few). Dorian gained very valuable knowledge and developed many meaningful connections. Dorian has had the opportunity to become a social justice trainer and continues to engage in the Breaking Barriers podcasts.

ITF Taekwondo

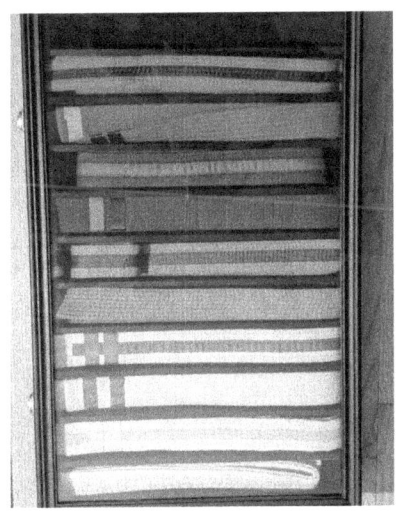

Dorian is also a martial artist and ITF Taekwondo practitioner. He has some knowledge of Isshin Ryu karate from his grandfather. Dorian Started ITF Taekwondo in May 2019. Through diligent and persistent work, he achieved a master's club affiliation. He also takes part in D.E.L.T.A. (Dedicated, Enthusiastic, Loyal, Teaching, Assistant) Team where he can assist in teaching and uplifting others' lives. Dorian is officially an Il-Dan and passionate about further training.

Thoughts Of Creativity King 114 Realities

Thoughts Of Creativity King 114 Realities is a creative self-help book. It is composed of unique free verse poetry, illustrations, haikus, and short stories. The purpose of this book is to help people cultivate themselves and think about their existence. The goal is to inspire people to make changes within themselves and others around them. Through free verse poetry, readers contemplate concepts of forgiveness, vulnerability, social issues, and goals. Illustrations bring an authentic and sincere visual aspect to the poetic work. Haikus add flavor of small implementation of imagery and meaning. The author also added short stories. These are personal stories from his life. These stories have moral and ethical lessons to help people overcome their troubles and misconceptions about life. This book took six years to produce. The work in this book comes heavily from experience. The experience comes from his own life and his perception of other people's condition, action, and mentality. Readers will learn from him and themselves by contemplating the literature and analyzing their reflection on their own life. This book allows people, young and old to read something relatable. The creative components will develop the reader's cravings for more. One goal for this book is to put it in the hands of the youth within schools nationwide. It will act as a supplement to poetry and storytelling in English classes. The book will ignite students' thinking about what kinds of topics can be discussed in the classroom. It will help students in developing their poetry. The beauty of poetry and storytelling within the classroom is that it assists in self-expression. In a sense, this book can be a tool to use as and develop coping mechanisms. When students are struggling with their emotions or expressing themselves, they can revert to this book, as a result, improving their emotional and mental well-being. This book is also suitable for creative writing programs, classes, and workshops. Dorian is working on his third book that will supersede the last books and all expectations.

Books Authored By Dorian S.Withrow Jr.

Book Alphabetical

Speak! Young Brown People, Speak. We are listening!
A.L. Savvy Publications 2014, 2022

Thoughts Of Creativity King 114 Realities. Dorian
Withrow Jr., Withrow LLC, Buffalo NY, 2022